Ericka & Morgan's Summer Vacation

The Imaginable Becomes Tangible

by: Frankie Perry

Gotham Books
30 N Gould St.
Ste. 20820, Sheridan, WY 82801
https://gothambooksinc.com/

Phone: 1 (307) 464-7800

© 2023 Frankie Perry. All rights reserved.

No part of this book may be reproduced, stored in a retrieval system, or transmitted by any means without the written permission of the author.

Published by Gotham Books (March 17, 2023)

ISBN: 979-8-88775-242-6 (sc)
ISBN: 979-8-88775-243-3 (e)

Because of the dynamic nature of the Internet, any web addresses or links contained in this book may have changed since publication and may no longer be valid.

The views expressed in this work are solely those of the author and do not necessarily reflect the views of the publisher, and the publisher hereby disclaims any responsibility for them.

This book is dedicated to:
My fellow members of the month plus 7 birthday club;
Joe, Kia and Morgan, I love y'all ❤

"The Dilemma"

Morgan had a notion fourth grade would be great

She was right, we made it! It's time to celebrate!

The Summer Break is upon us and time to have fun

And of course, as my bestie, Morgan's my plus one

My birthday is actually the 4th of July

My parents have promised me, my limit is the sky

Whatever I want they gave me total carte blanche

I could literally choose to watch a rocket launch

But since Morgan and I will vacation as a set
I asked her for some ideas that we both could vet
Her first thought was a visit to the brand-new zoo
Exhibiting exotic animals like the tree-kangaroo
Next, she mentioned a summer festival and fair
Saying "I'm sure the two of us could have fun there"
With corn dogs and cotton candy and prizes to win
Face painting, dunking booths, watching aerialist spin

"The Imaginable Becomes Tangible"

Well, Ericka J, wasn't too keen on those suggestions
Reminding Morgan of her clear physical exceptions
"This is not school, there's no 504's nor any IEP
The real world isn't always accommodating to me
I'm not asking for a pity party", EJ said then sighed
"But there's nothing at the carnival for me to ride...

...Inaccessibility is one of two things I really dread
The other is a condescending pat on my head"
Though Morgan's IQ score is through the roof
She admitted her ideas were somewhat aloof
So, she looked EJ in her emerald-green eyes
And choked up just a little as she apologized

Sitting in the kitchen was Auntie Brynn Brynn

And so was Mr. Melvin, her longtime boyfriend

The girls didn't know the two had overheard them

Until a great suggestion came from Uncle M

"I have the perfect solution for your vacation

There are mobility camps all over the nation

That accommodate kids with crutches or wheelchairs

Let's look for the best one and we'll get y'all there"

"Let me offer an explanation because of my A D D
sometimes my thoughts just get ahead of me"
They all assured Morgan not to feel bad
They knew she didn't intend to make Ericka sad
With renewed excitement the girls expressed delight
The pair grabbed their devices to search for campsites

They searched and searched until those two found
No Limits LLC, a perfectly awesome campground
The last week in June would definitely work out
Then home back in time for Uncle Sam's cook-out
Though the three-week wait seemed an eternity away
Finally, they arrived at that destination day

The parents dropped them off at the welcome sign
With luggage in tow, they stood in a very long line
Morgan impulsively yelled "please open the gate"
"Two more minutes young lady… it's only 7:58"
Two minutes, she was thinking, would take forever
But sooner than later the guard lifted the brass lever

They looked at brochures while eating eggs and bacon
There was no time to waste with all that decision-making
They studied the agenda for all the scheduled events
And decided on which activities they'd be participants
After breakfast they socialized in a 'let's meet and greet'
As the campers decided how they would all compete

The girls challenged two boys to a game of ping pong

Feeling with table tennis they could not go wrong

Isaiah and Punkin were both up for that same task

But before the game began, Ericka just had to ask

"Is that your nick name or are you really named Punkin?"

He answered with a question, "are donuts for dunking?"

After story telling with puppets, day one was complete
But before the two of them would dare fall asleep
They facetimed their parents as they promised they would
And recalled the day's events as being beyond good
Ericka even shared how the camp made her feel
Recalling detailed modifications, just like a highlight reel

Early the next morning at the break of the second day

After a hearty breakfast it was again time to play

They partnered with Isaiah and Punkin once more

Tossing bean bags into corn holes just for those four

In the afternoon the campers came out full force

As all of them competed in an obstacle course

Morgan tripped and fell, skinning her left knee

Ericka grabbed her hand saying "come ride with me"

So, Morgan hopped up on her bestie pooh's lap

Ericka maneuvered the course, as if she had a map

Unfortunately, those two did not win that race

But the lost was no cause for any disgrace

Ericka and Morgan were having fun galore

And who could be sad while toasting S'mores?

So, another camp day had come and gone

And as expected the girls grabbed their phones

Keeping family updated about their awesome vacation

Sharing stories about campers from across the nation

"Today Aunt Brynn-Brynn we were fishing off the pier
Morgan and I are having a total blast down here!
The lifeguard on duty was Coach Raquel Euzelle
She gave us fake fish bait made of glowing gel
As we were fishing, we watched the butterflies swarm
And the most beautiful Monarch landed on my arm
Our counselors helped us catch fish then release."
Aunt Brynn was feeling ecstatic for her niece

The design of the camp was simply unbelievable
Making challenging activities quite conceivable
Open-minded architects full of good intentions
Resulted in a great camp with witty inventions
While on crutches, in a wheelchair or walking outright
Every individual enrolled could enjoy this campsite

She summarized the experience embracing this mentality;
The other campers and she shared a strong commonality
Be it 'Simon Says' or a treasure hunt everyone could join in
Or the wheelchair basketball games where any team could win
It was during the tournament that they met Coach Dwayne
He did trick shots and dribbling combos that looked so insane
Maneuvering his wheelchair like a professional ice-skater
He defied all the odds and astounded any would-be haters

Camp No Limits was literally a non-restrictive play world
Not just for those on crutches, but for every boy and girl
The activities throughout the week were the camper's choice
But the finale was mandatory unlike the softball toss
The camp counselors had planned an 'end-of-camp dance'
Giving them the opportunity to mingle, one final chance
Lovelier than any prom ever thought of or ever seen
Better than a quinceañera, wedding or sweet sixteen
It had nothing to do with a coordinated choreography
Just an individual expression of each camper's mobility

It was finally time to say goodbye, to a really fantastic stay
As all the No Limits campers went their individual way
The parting friends agreed that the experience was very sweet
Enough so that they vowed that they would annually meet
Ericka and Morgan returned home and they fondly recalled
The memories from the campsite that left them enthralled

The next thing you know it was Independence Day
And if you will recall, Ericka Jestine's birthday
Her party was phenomenal with all the family there
Sharing BBQ and birthday cake (an unlikely pair!)
The fireworks lit up the sky just like Rudolph's nose
Melvin got on one knee and there he did propose
Before Aunt Brynn Brynn could utter a "yes"
The entire family accepted, unofficially, in jest
Ericka looked at her bestie and gleefully said
"Next step Morgan, we'll be junior bridesmaids"

Before Summer vacation ended for these Georgia Peaches

They had sleep overs with friends at two different beaches

They watched movies and ate popcorn topped with cheddar cheese

And threw frisbees for their pets whenever there was a breeze

On weekends they prepped Mason jars for Granny's fruit canning

And Brynn Brynn included them with some of her wedding planning

Unfortunately, all good times come to an end, no surprise

It was now time to shop for school uniforms and supplies

They were optimistic this school year would turn out to be super

And hopeful that their new teacher would be as great as

Ms. Cooper!

www.ingramcontent.com/pod-product-compliance
Lightning Source LLC
LaVergne TN
LVHW061957070526
838199LV00060B/4181